DATE:

LOCATION:

VALUE:

ITEMS FOUND:

NOTES:

DATE:

LOCATION:

VALUE:

ITEMS FOUND:

NOTES:

Date:

Location:

Value:

Items found:

Notes:

DATE:

LOCATION:

VALUE:

ITEMS FOUND:

NOTES:

Date:

Location:

Value:

Items
Found:

Notes:

DATE:

LOCATION:

VALUE:

ITEMS FOUND:

NOTES:

Date:

Location:

Value:

Items Found:

Notes:

DATE:

LOCATION:

VALUE:

ITEMS FOUND:

NOTES:

Date:

Location:

Value:

Items Found:

Notes:

Date:

Location:

Value:

Items
Found:

Notes:

Date:

Location:

Value:

Items
Found:

Notes:

DATE:

LOCATION:

VALUE:

ITEMS FOUND:

NOTES:

Date:

Location:

Value:

Items Found:

Notes:

DATE:

LOCATION:

VALUE:

ITEMS FOUND:

NOTES:

DATE:

LOCATION:

VALUE:

ITEMS FOUND:

NOTES:

DATE:

LOCATION:

VALUE:

ITEMS FOUND:

NOTES:

Date:

Location:

Value:

Items Found:

Notes:

Date:

Location:

Value:

Items Found:

Notes:

DATE:

LOCATION:

VALUE:

ITEMS FOUND:

NOTES:

DATE:

LOCATION:

VALUE:

ITEMS FOUND:

NOTES:

Date:

Location:

Value:

Items found:

Notes:

DATE:

LOCATION:

VALUE:

ITEMS FOUND:

NOTES:

Date:

Location:

Value:

Items Found:

Notes:

DATE:

LOCATION:

VALUE:

ITEMS FOUND:

NOTES:

DATE:

LOCATION:

VALUE:

ITEMS FOUND:

NOTES:

Date:

Location:

Value:

Items
Found:

Notes:

Date:

Location:

Value:

Items found:

Notes:

DATE:

LOCATION:

VALUE:

ITEMS FOUND:

NOTES:

Date:

Location:

Value:

Items found:

Notes:

DATE:

LOCATION:

VALUE:

ITEMS FOUND:

NOTES:

DATE:

LOCATION:

VALUE:

ITEMS FOUND:

NOTES:

DATE:

LOCATION:

VALUE:

ITEMS FOUND:

NOTES:

Date:

Location:

Value:

Items found:

Notes:

DATE:

LOCATION:

VALUE:

ITEMS FOUND:

NOTES:

Date:

Location:

Value:

Items
Found:

Notes:

DATE:

LOCATION:

VALUE:

ITEMS FOUND:

NOTES:

DATE:

LOCATION:

VALUE:

ITEMS FOUND:

NOTES:

DATE:

LOCATION:

VALUE:

ITEMS FOUND:

NOTES:

Date:

Location:

Value:

Items found:

Notes:

DATE:

LOCATION:

VALUE:

ITEMS FOUND:

NOTES:

DATE:

LOCATION:

VALUE:

ITEMS FOUND:

NOTES:

Date:

Location:

Value:

Items Found:

Notes:

Date:

Location:

Value:

Items Found:

Notes:

Date:

Location:

Value:

Items Found:

Notes:

Date:

Location:

Value:

Items found:

Notes:

DATE:

LOCATION:

VALUE:

ITEMS FOUND:

NOTES:

Date:

Location:

Value:

Items found:

Notes:

DATE:

LOCATION:

VALUE:

ITEMS FOUND:

NOTES:

Date:

Location:

Value:

Items Found:

Notes:

DATE:

LOCATION:

VALUE:

ITEMS FOUND:

NOTES:

DATE:

LOCATION:

VALUE:

ITEMS FOUND:

NOTES:

DATE:

LOCATION:

VALUE:

ITEMS FOUND:

NOTES:

DATE:

LOCATION:

VALUE:

ITEMS FOUND:

NOTES:

DATE:

LOCATION:

VALUE:

ITEMS FOUND:

NOTES:

DATE:

LOCATION:

VALUE:

ITEMS FOUND:

NOTES:

DATE:

LOCATION:

VALUE:

ITEMS FOUND:

NOTES:

Date:

Location:

Value:

Items found:

Notes:

DATE:

LOCATION:

VALUE:

ITEMS FOUND:

NOTES:

Date:

Location:

Value:

Items found:

Notes:

DATE:

LOCATION:

VALUE:

ITEMS FOUND:

NOTES:

DATE:

LOCATION:

VALUE:

ITEMS FOUND:

NOTES:

Date:

Location:

Value:

Items Found:

Notes:

DATE:

LOCATION:

VALUE:

ITEMS FOUND:

NOTES:

DATE:

LOCATION:

VALUE:

ITEMS FOUND:

NOTES:

Date:

Location:

Value:

Items Found:

Notes:

Date:

Location:

Value:

Items found:

Notes:

DATE:

LOCATION:

VALUE:

ITEMS
FOUND:

NOTES:

DATE:

LOCATION:

VALUE:

ITEMS FOUND:

NOTES:

DATE:

LOCATION:

VALUE:

ITEMS FOUND:

NOTES:

DATE:

LOCATION:

VALUE:

ITEMS FOUND:

NOTES:

DATE:

LOCATION:

VALUE:

ITEMS FOUND:

NOTES:

DATE:

LOCATION:

VALUE:

ITEMS FOUND:

NOTES:

Date:

Location:

Value:

Items found:

Notes:

DATE:

LOCATION:

VALUE:

ITEMS FOUND:

NOTES:

Date:

Location:

Value:

Items found:

Notes:

Date:

Location:

Value:

Items found:

Notes:

Date:

Location:

Value:

Items Found:

Notes:

Date:

Location:

Value:

Items Found:

Notes:

Date:

Location:

Value:

Items found:

Notes:

DATE:

LOCATION:

VALUE:

ITEMS FOUND:

NOTES:

Date:

Location:

Value:

Items found:

Notes:

DATE:

LOCATION:

VALUE:

ITEMS FOUND:

NOTES:

Date:

Location:

Value:

Items found:

Notes:

Date:

Location:

Value:

Items found:

Notes:

Date:

Location:

Value:

Items Found:

Notes:

Date:

Location:

Value:

Items Found:

Notes:

Date:

Location:

Value:

Items found:

Notes:

Date:

Location:

Value:

Items found:

Notes:

Date:

Location:

Value:

Items Found:

Notes:

Date:

Location:

Value:

Items
found:

Notes:

DATE:

LOCATION:

VALUE:

ITEMS FOUND:

NOTES:

DATE:

LOCATION:

VALUE:

ITEMS FOUND:

NOTES:

Date:

Location:

Value:

Items found:

Notes:

Date:

Location:

Value:

Items Found:

Notes:

Date:

Location:

Value:

Items Found:

Notes:

DATE:

LOCATION:

VALUE:

ITEMS FOUND:

NOTES:

Date:

Location:

Value:

Items found:

Notes:

Date:

Location:

Value:

Items found:

Notes:

Date:

Location:

Value:

Items found:

Notes:

Date:

Location:

Value:

Items found:

Notes:

Date:

Location:

Value:

Items found:

Notes:

DATE:

LOCATION:

VALUE:

ITEMS FOUND:

NOTES:

DATE:

LOCATION:

VALUE:

ITEMS FOUND:

NOTES:

DATE:

LOCATION:

VALUE:

ITEMS FOUND:

NOTES:

DATE:

LOCATION:

VALUE:

ITEMS FOUND:

NOTES:

DATE:

LOCATION:

VALUE:

ITEMS FOUND:

NOTES:

Date:

Location:

Value:

Items
Found:

Notes:

DATE:

LOCATION:

VALUE:

ITEMS FOUND:

NOTES:

Date:

Location:

Value:

Items Found:

Notes:

DATE:

LOCATION:

VALUE:

ITEMS FOUND:

NOTES:

Date:

Location:

Value:

Items found:

Notes:

Date:

Location:

Value:

Items found:

Notes:

Date:

Location:

Value:

Items found:

Notes:

DATE:

LOCATION:

VALUE:

ITEMS FOUND:

NOTES:

DATE:

LOCATION:

VALUE:

ITEMS FOUND:

NOTES:

DATE:

LOCATION:

VALUE:

ITEMS FOUND:

NOTES:

Date:

Location:

Value:

Items found:

Notes:

Made in the USA
Las Vegas, NV
25 November 2022

Date:

Location:

Value:

Items Found:

Notes: